THE HISTORY OF TRAP

ERIC REESE

Copyright © 2022 by Eric Reese

All rights reserved.

No part of this book may be reproduced in any form or by any electronic or mechanical means, including information storage and retrieval systems, without written permission from the author, except for the use of brief quotations in a book review.

CONTENTS

What is Trap?	1
Origins of Trap	4
Subgenres Of Trap	13
Fusion Trap and its genres	31
Notable Trap Albums to Date	46
Afterword	61
If you didn't know	63
The Golden Age	64
World Hip Hop	66
Across the World	70
Glitch Hop and Wonky Music	73
Crunk and Snap Music	75
What to read next…	77

WHAT IS TRAP?

The trap is a hip-hop subgenre that arose in the early 2000s in the southern United States. The term "trap" comes from an Atlanta slang term that refers to a residence that is only used to distribute narcotics. Complex hi-hat rhythms, tuned kick drums with a lengthy decay (initially from the Roland TR-808 drum machine), and lyrical material that typically focuses on drug addiction and urban violence define trap music, which employs synthetic drums. It only uses a few instruments, virtually entirely comprising of snare drums and double- or triple-timed hi-hats.

Producers Kurtis Mantronik, Mannie Fresh, Shawty Redd, Zaytoven, Fatboi, DJ Screw, and Toomp, as well as artists Young Jeezy, Gucci Mane, and T.I., are all pioneers of the genre (who coined the term with his

2003 album Trap Muzik). Producer Lex Luger, who cofounded the successful hip-hop production company 808 Mafia and created the groundbreaking WakaFlocka Flame album *Flockaveli* in 2010, pioneered the current trap sound.

The trap has become one of the most popular forms of American music since breaking into the mainstream in the 2010s, consistently dominating the Billboard Hot 100 throughout the decade, with artists like Drake, Future, Cardi B, Migos, Lil Uzi Vert, Post Malone, XXXTentacion, Young Thug, and Travis Scott (among many others) all achieving No. 1s on the chart with songs featuring trap-inspired production.

It has influenced many pop and R&B musicians, including Ariana Grande, Beyoncé, Miley Cyrus, Rihanna, and others. Reggaetón and K-pop are examples of its impact. According to Nielsen Data, hip-hop became the most popular style of music for the first time in 2018, coinciding with trap's sustained success. In 2019, Lil Nas X's trap-inspired country/rap crossover "Old Town Road" (with Billy Ray Cyrus) set a new record for the most weeks (19) at No. 1 on the Billboard Hot 100 chart, as well as the fastest single to achieve Diamond Certification.

Characteristics

Lyrical topics in trap music must focus around life and culture in the "trap" or in a real southern "trap house" where drugs are peddled. The terminology "trap" refers to a location where drugs are sold. Street life, getting riches, crime, cars, and struggles that artists have had in their southern American settings are among the other subjects covered. If the "trap" isn't mentioned in the song, it isn't considered "trap" music.

Crisp, grimy, and rhythmic snares, deep 808 kick drums, double-time, triple-time, and similarly divided hi-hats, and cinematic and symphonic use of string, brass, woodwind, and keyboard instruments are used to create an energetic, hard-hitting, deep, and varied atmosphere in trap music. Producer Shawty Redd is responsible for these key features, which have become the hallmark sound of trap music. Trap beats can be as slow as 50 B.P.M. (coded at 100 BPM for finer hi-hat subdivision) or as fast as 88 (176) B.P.M., although the average trap beat is about 70 (140) B.P.M.

ORIGINS OF TRAP

The 1990s–2003: Origins

Lil Jon from Atlanta, Georgia, where the term "trap" originated as a reference to places where drug deals are made, worked with local Atlanta acts such as Dungeon Family, Outkast, Goodie Mob, Three 6 Mafia, and Ghetto Mafia, as well as Mannie Fresh from New Orleans and DJ Paul from Memphis, Tennessee. U.G.K.'s "Cocaine In The Back of the Ride" from their first E.P., "The Southern Way," was one of the first tracks to be released in 1992.

They released "Pocket Full of Stones" off their major-label debut album Too Hard to Swallow later in 1992. It was also used in the film Menace II Society, which was released in 1993. Master P's song "Mr. Ice Cream Man" off his fifth studio album, Ice Cream Man, was released in 1996.

Rappers whose major lyrical focus was drug dealing began to be referred to as "trap rappers" by fans and critics. The words "the dope boyz in the trap nigga / the thug nigga, drug dealer where you at" appear in T.I.'s 2001 song "Dope Boyz" from his first album I'm Serious. "The trap in the early 2000s wasn't a genre. It was a genuine location," noted Complex's David Drake, and the phrase was eventually used to describe the "music created about that area."

2003–2015: Rise in mainstream popularity

After the popular success of several albums and songs with lyrics about life in "the trap," drug selling, and the battle for success in the early to mid-2000s, trap music developed as a recognized genre. T.I., Young Jeezy, Gucci Mane, Boosie Badazz, Young Dolph, Lil Wayne, and Rick Ross, all of whom had drug dealer personas, produced crossover hits and helped to expand the popularity of the genre, with trap records appearing more frequently on mixtapes and radio stations outside of the South.

Though trap artists' production methods varied, the trademark and archetypal trap sound (usually built on synth, orchestra, and string swells with tight, bass-heavy

808 kick beats) evolved in Atlanta during the genre's mid-2000s breakthrough. DJ Toomp, Fatboi, Drumma Boy, Shawty Redd, D. Rich, and Zaytoven are some of the most well-known trap producers from the mid-to-late 2000s. Earlier Southern producers like Lil Jon, Mannie Fresh, and DJ Paul inspired the first wave of trap music.

From T.I.: "Except for Outkast, let me remember, Goodie Mob, it was Lil Jon, Outkast, Goodie Mob, right, so you had crunk music, and you had Organized Noize before I got into the game. There was no such thing as trap music until I invented it, then I invented it again. Trap Muzik, my second album, was released in 2003, and I was the one who originated the word. Following that, a whole new musical genre arose. An open lane for each of you to do what you want and live your life on television while being welcomed by the general public. Because I opened the door and you stepped through it, the people have accepted you. Remember who it was who opened the door."

By the end of the decade, a new generation of trap musicians had emerged, and they were regularly topping the Billboard hip hop charts. Lex Luger, a prominent trap producer, created over 200 tracks in 2010 and 2011, including several hits for major rap, acts, like Rick Ross' "B.M.F. (Blowin' Money Fast)."

THE HISTORY OF TRAP

Luger's characteristic trap sound has featured 808s, sharp snares, quick hi-hats, synth keys, and orchestration of brass, violins, woodwinds, and keyboards since his ascent to fame. Other hip-hop producers have copied many of his sounds in an attempt to duplicate his popularity. Luger is frequently credited for popularizing the contemporary trap sound because of this. Since the 2010s, a slew of new trap producers has risen to prominence, including Southside and TM88 of the 808 Mafia, Sonny Digital, Young Chop, DJ Spinz, Tay Keith, and Metro Boomin. Some producers branched out into different genres, including current R&B (Mike WiLL Made-It) and electronic music (Araab Muzik).

With several tracks recorded by rappers such as Young Jeezy, Chief Keef, and Future, trap music maintained a significant presence on the mainstream Billboard music charts during 2011 and 2012. Jeezy's single "Ballin" peaked at number 57 on the Billboard charts and was widely regarded as one of his greatest songs in a long time.

Future's track "Turn On the Lights" was certified gold and reached number 50 on the Billboard Hot 100, while Keef's "I Don't Like" and "Love Sosa" had over 30 million views on YouTube, introducing a new trap subgenre known as the drill. Drill production style has been dubbed the "sonic cousin of nervous footwork, southern-fried hip-hop, and the 808 trigger-finger of trap" by music reviewers.

Young Chop is cited by critics as the most representative producer of the genre. The drill is heavily influenced by trap producer Lex Luger's music. Young Chop cites Shawty Redd, Drumma Boy, and Zaytoven as essential forerunners to the drill style. Kanye West, a fellow Chicago native, and well-known hip hop producer and rapper, remixed "I Don't Like," which was included on his label GOOD Music's compilation album Cruel Summer. Trap music has been dubbed "the sound of hip hop in 2012" by G.Q.'s Stelios Phili.

Trap music has influenced non-hip-hop artists since it has maintained a significant presence on the mainstream music charts. The songs "Drunk in Love," "Flawless," and "7/11" by R&B artist Beyoncé, all from her 2013 album Beyoncé, all had trap influences. Lady Gaga collaborated with rappers T.I., Too Short, and Twista on a trap-inspired song named "Jewels 'n Drugs" for her 2013 album Art Pop. Critics reacted to the fusion of pop and trapped music with conflicting feelings. Katy Perry's song "Dark Horse," which featured rapper Juicy J and was taken from her 2013 album Prism, was released in September 2013 and featured trap elements. By the end of January 2014, the song has climbed to the top of the Billboard Hot 100.

2015–present: Expansion and mainstream ubiquity

New Jersey rapper FettyWap's hit single "Trap Queen" peaked at number two on the U.S. Billboard Hot 100 chart in May 2015, bringing trap music back to the top of mainstream music charts. "My Way" and "679," FettyWap's succeeding singles, also charted in the top ten on the Billboard Hot 100 chart.

Desiigner, a Brooklyn-based rapper, rose to prominence in 2016 after his debut mixtape single, "Panda," topped the U.S. Billboard Hot 100 chart. Internet memes aided the commercial success of trap songs, as was the case with Rae Sremmurd and Gucci Mane's "Black Beatles," which reached number one on the Billboard Hot 100 chart after being exposed through the internet phenomena known as the "Mannequin Challenge."

Similarly, Migos and Lil Uzi Vert's duet "Bad and Boujee" reached number one in 2017 after internet meme exposure, including the now-famous lyrics "Raindrop (Drip), Droptop (Drop Top)." In June 2017, 2 Chainz released his fourth studio album, Pretty Girls Like Trap Music. Cardi B rose to prominence after her song "Bodak Yellow" reached number one on the Billboard Hot 100 in 2017.

Producer D.J. Snake popularized trap-influenced E.D.M., which became popular in 2013.

In 2015, the term "Latin trap" was used to describe a new fusion of trap music. Latin trap is similar to mainstream trap because it focuses on "'la Calle,' or the streets, and includes hustling sex and narcotics. Bryant Myers, Anuel AA, Miky Woodz, Almighty, Maluma, and Bad Bunny are some of the most well-known Latin trap performers. "Rappers from Puerto Rico have taken parts of trap—the lurching bass lines, jittering 808s, and the eyes-half-closed vibe—and injected them into banger after banger," The Fader said in July 2017.

In an August 2017 piece for Billboard's "A Brief History Of" series, they gathered the help of some of the genre's biggest names, including Ozuna, De La Ghetto, Bad Bunny, Farruko, and Arcangel, to tell the story of Latin trap. "[Jorge] Fonseca featured Puerto Rican musicians including Anuel AA, Bryant Myers, and Noriel on the compilation Trap Capos: Season 1, which became the first "Latin trap" L.P. to hit number one on Billboard's Latin Rhythm Albums chart," according to Elias Leight of Rolling Stone.

Cardi B's single "Bodak Yellow" (which had previously reached number one on the U.S. Billboard Hot 100 list) was remixed and released on August 18, 2017, as the "Latin Trap Remix," which features Cardi B rapping in Spanish and Dominican hip hop recording artist Messiah delivering a guest verse. "A growing Latin trap sound is responding to more recent trends as it combines

THE HISTORY OF TRAP

with Reggaeton, embracing the slow-rolling rhythms and gooey vocal delivery favored by Southern hip-hop," Rolling Stone stated in November 2017.

A "booming, trap-laden" sound with "flavorful" parts and mumble rap make up "bubblegum rap." It's also been dubbed "ushering in a new generation of Internet-borne music stars."

* * *

Childish Gambino released "This Is America" on May 5, 2018, a song "based on the sharp contrast between joyful, syncretic melodies and ominous trap cadences." It debuted at number one on the Billboard Charts and received over 65 million streams in its first week.

T.I. opened a pop-up Trap Music Museum in Atlanta in 2018 to promote his album Dime Trap: "From the beginning, we were in charge of curating it. Its goal was to honor the culture's most important contributors. Second, educate others who may not be familiar with the genre. And they should encourage individuals who are in the genre's surroundings." 'Escape the Trap,' a museum escape room, is also available.

Ariana Grande, an American pop-R&B singer, included trap influences on her fourth studio album, Sweetener, released in 2018 while preserving her characteristic pop-

R&B sound. From her fifth studio album Thank U, Next, she expanded on trap experimentation with songs like "7 Rings," "Bad Idea," "In My Head," and "Break Up with Your Girlfriend, I'm Bored." Sweetener and Thank U, Next was both critical and financial successes, with the former earning the Grammy Award for Best Pop Vocal Album and the latter breaking many streaming records and spawning two Billboard Hot 100 number one songs. Positions, Grande's sixth studio album, is primarily a trap-inspired R&B-pop album.

Lil Nas X's "Old Town Road" merged trap, Western, and country music in 2019. The song debuted at number 19 on the Hot Country Songs list in March 2019 before being pulled a week later. On April 5, 2019, a remix featuring Billy Ray Cyrus was released, and it went on to become the longest-running number-one hip-hop single of all time, as well as the overall longest number-one single of all time on the Billboard Hot 100, with 19 weeks, surpassing Mariah Carey and Boyz II Men's "One Sweet Day" and Luis Fonsi and Daddy Yankee's "Despacito" featuring Justin Bieber's previous records.

SUBGENRES OF TRAP

Cloud rap

Cloud rap is a hazy, dreamy, and relaxing subgenre of Southern rap and traps music that includes various Lo-Fi musical characteristics. Many music experts regard Lil B, a rapper, and Clams Casino, a producer, as the early pioneers of this genre. The phrase "cloud rap" refers to the genre's internet origins and ethereal sound.

Origins

During the late 2000s, Atlanta, Houston, and Memphis were the birthplaces of cloud rap. Cloud rap elements, such as Lo-Fi and dreamy atmospheres, may be heard on Clouddead's self-titled album from 2001. Viper's second album, Ready...and Willing, released later in 2006, contains more building elements, such as hazy and relaxed sounds. Some have given the word to rapper Lil B.

In a 2009 article, music journalist Noz said that rapper Lil B showed him a CGI image of a castle in the clouds and remarked, "That's the kind of music I want to make," claiming that Lil B coined the word. Clams Casino is also credited with pioneering the cloud rap sound through collaborations with Lil B as early as 2010.

3 Years Ahead: The Cloud Rap Tape, a compilation of tracks from the Space Age Hustle blog, used the term as well. The album is made up of songs that are classified as cloud rap. With rapper A$AP Rocky's debut mixtape, Live. Love, the genre, gained popular prominence in 2011. A$ A.P.

The term "cloud rap" is commonly used to describe foggy, Lo-Fi rap.

Characteristics

Cloud rap has a similar rhythm to Lo-Fi and chill-wave, but distorted, hallucinogenic samples and the use of rap distinguish it. Cloud computing's "diversity of inspirations and ease accessibility" serves as inspiration for the genre. Hip hop, drum and bass, grime, and trip-hop, as well as R&B, dance, indie, rock, and pop music genres, have influenced him.

The name "cloud" refers to the genre's "hazy," ethereal look (in terms of both aural and visual representation) as well as its ambiguity as a genre with no clearly defined bounds. The lyrics of cloud rap often deal with themes of love and betrayal, as well as more common subjects in popular music like sex, drugs, and isolation. Nonsensical catchphrases and Twitter baits, such as "swag" and "based," are frequently used by vocalists, highlighting a feeling of self-aware ridiculousness as an attempt at parody while embracing the origins of online culture.

Cloud rap draws on a wide range of rap sounds and locations, including the East and West Coast, as well as the South. In particular, it frequently employs looping samples from female singers, particularly those whose voices have an ethereal feel. Also, it is frequently released without the involvement of record labels. Its rap artists rely on online services to distribute and promote their music (such as SoundCloud, YouTube, and Twitter).

Artists and producers

Clams Casino contributed three tracks to Lil B's mixtape 6 Kiss, which was released in 2009. Clams Casino aided A$AP Rocky in the production of Live. Love.in 2011. With 1,164,114 listeners, A$ A.P. has one of the most popular mixtapes in cloud rap. The mixtape features classic cloud rap characteristics and themes like drug usage, sex, and self-reflection, among others.

Imogen Heap, like Clams Casino, debuted in this genre in 2009, with Clams Casino sampling her music on Lil B's song "I'm God." Lil B has sampled Heap several times since then. Heap solidified her place in the cloud rap genre by appearing on *Live. Love.A$AP Rocky* in 2011.

In 2013, when the video for his tune "Ginseng Strip 2002" went viral, Swedish rapper Yung Lean rose to prominence as a leading cloud rap artist. By mainly adopting a sad, dreamy rapping style, Yung Lean shifted the more modern version of cloud rap to a "free-for-all zone," departing slightly from conventional cloud rap sounds.

Post Malone, XXXTentacion and Lil Peep, $uicideboy$, and Bones are among the other well-known cloud rap musicians.

While the music of these artists falls under a variety of other genres such as trap, Lo-Fi, and hip hop, they have all recorded tracks with cloud rap features such as slower rapping, ethereal music, and lyrics about drugs and sex.

Drill music

THE HISTORY OF TRAP

A drill is a trap music genre characterized by its ominous trap-influenced beats and dark, aggressive, and nihilistic lyrical content.

Drill gained popularity in the United States in mid-2012 and thanks to the success of rappers and producers like Chief Keef, Lil Durk, Lil Reese, Fredo Santana, Young Chop, G Herbo, Lil Bibby, and King Louie, who had a large fanbase in their home country and a strong online presence. Drill performers were signed to major labels after receiving media exposure. Artists in the genre are known for their lyricism and links to crime in Chicago.

Beginning in 2012, a regional subgenre of U.K. drill evolved in London, mainly in the Brixton neighborhood. By the mid-2010s, the U.K. drill had become well known, influencing other regional scenes such as Australian, Spanish, Irish, Dutch, and Brooklyn drills (re-introduced to Brooklyn in the late 2010s).

Characteristics

Drill's lyrics are typically harsh and gritty. "Nihilistic drill represents real reality where its squeaky-clean hip-hop contemporaries have failed," Lucy Stehlik of The Guardian wrote. Drill songs stand in stark contrast to the subject matter of earlier Chicago rappers and present mainstream hip hop, which tended to praise and celebrate riches at the time of drill's release.

Drill lyrics are often nasty, brutal, realistic, and nihilistic, reflecting life on the streets. Drill rappers have a dismal, deadpan delivery influenced by the "stoned, aimless warbling of Soulja Boy (one of the initial non-local Keef partners) and Lil Wayne before him," which is typically filtered through Auto-Tune. Gucci Mane and Waka Flocka Flame, both from Atlanta, were major inspirations for the drill culture. Despite its resemblance to trap music, a drill beat's tempo is often slower, with a moderate tempo of 60 to 70 beats per minute. Some producers operate at a faster speed, like 120 to 140 beats per minute.

Drillers are typically young; many of the scene's most well-known musicians rose to prominence while still in their teens. Chief Keef, one of the genre's most well-known musicians, was 16 when he secured a multi-million dollar record deal with Interscope, while Lil Wayne co-signed Lil Mouse, a 13-year-old driller. Drill rappers' lack of regard for metaphor or wordplay has been observed by critics.

Chief Keef explained that his straightforward flow is a deliberate aesthetic choice: "I'm quite aware of what I'm doing. I was able to master it. I don't even employ analogies or punchlines because I'm not required to. But I might be able to... That, in my opinion, is excessive. I'd rather just express what's happening right now. I'm not a big fan of metaphors or jokes like that." What

THE HISTORY OF TRAP

Moser said about Keef's songs "They feel cramped and airless since they are lyrically, rhythmically [sic], and emotionally depleted... It's not even fatalistic because it would imply self-awareness, a moral consideration, which the lyrics don't include. It simply is, over and over."

With few exceptions, this music is unadulterated, raw, and devoid of bright areas, with an emphasis on rage and violence. The natural reaction is to label this music as harsh, merciless, and concrete-hard, but it's actually jubilant in its darkness. Most of its practitioners are young and emerging into their own creative selves against a backdrop of heinous violence in Chicago, particularly among young people—dozens of youngsters have been killed this year—and often linked to gangs. (Chicago's gangs and Chicago's rap have a long history of colliding.)

Since the beginning, female artists have been represented in the scene. According to Miles Raymer of Pitchfork, "Instead of rapping about being a 'Hitta,' they rapped about being in love with hittas, the local term for a shooter. Aside from that, they used the same icy sociopathic sounds from the same producers as any other drill rappers, and they came across as equally tough." In their songs, female drillers mix themes of violence and love; according to Katie Got Bandz, "Males would not anticipate a girl to rap about drilling, so it's unique. Females selling themselves is nothing new to them."

Drill production is the "sonic cousin of nervous footwork, southern-fried hip-hop, and the 808 trigger-finger of trap," according to Stehlik. Young Chop is cited by critics as the most representative producer of the genre. A drill is heavily influenced by trap producer Lex Luger's music, and Young Chop cites Shawty Redd, Drumma Boy, and Zaytoven as notable drill forerunners.

History

Drill, according to Complex's David Drake, is defined by "the entirety of the culture: the terminology, the dances, the mentality, and the music, much of which originated in 'Dro City,' a gang-designated region of city blocks in the Woodlawn neighborhood."

"Drill" implies to fight or counterattack in street slang and "may be used for anything from females getting dolled up to the all-out street battle." Pacman, a rapper from Dro City, is credited with being the first to apply the word to local hip-hop music. He is considered the stylistic inventor of the genre.

Drake defined the drill scene as a grassroots movement that had hatched in a closed, interlocking system: on the streets and on social media in a network of clubs and parties, as well as among high schools, during the early

2010s ascent of Chicago hip hop. Amid growing violence and a homicide crisis, a drill was designed on Chicago's South Side.

"A shift from historic feuding between monolithic crime organizations controlling thousands of members each to intrapersonal squabbling and retaliatory conflicts among smaller hybrid groups whose control extends only a few blocks... The toughened reality of living in these neighborhoods is what shaped Drill music," according to Mark Guarino of Salon. Rap and gang warfare collide in the drill culture, and many of the young rappers have had prior experience with violence. Chief Keef "represents both a dangerous strain of modern hip hop culture and a genuinely alienated group within American society," according to Sam Gould of The Independent.

Drill musicians were collaborating with rappers from various scenes and hip hop icons like Kanye West, Drake, and Rick Ross by late 2012. For the 2012 GOOD Music compilation Cruel Summer, Kanye West remixed "I Don't Like" as "Don't Like," featuring West, Chief Keef, Pusha T, Big Sean, and Jadakiss. The drill had a major influence on West's 2013 album *Yeezus*, which also contained vocals from Chief Keef and King Louie.

Drill's subject matter is very different from that of Kid Sister, Lupe Fiasco, Psalm One, Rhymefest, and The Cool Kids, who were all from Chicago.

Drill's success and aggressiveness have elicited varied reactions from older Chicago rappers. Lupe Fiasco, a musician, remarked in a radio broadcast, "Chief Keef gives me the creeps. It's not so much him as it is the society he represents... The murder rate in Chicago is on the rise, and you can see who's behind it: they all look like Chief Keef." Fiasco revealed he was considering leaving the music industry after Chief Keef threatened him on Twitter. The drill is "the theme music to murder," according to Rhymefest.

While Chicago drill music faded from the widespread appeal, a new scene arose in the United Kingdom, which by the late-2010s had swept across Europe, encouraging the formation of drill scenes across the continent. Compared to the Chicago drill, the U.K. drill developed its own particular style of production. Bobby Shmurda and Rowdy Rebel, two Chicago-influenced Brooklyn drill musicians, emerged in the mid-2010s, while Pop Smoke, Sheff G, Fivio Foreign, Sleepy Hallow, and 22Gz emerged in the late-2010s as new renowned drill artists from Brooklyn.

Artists including Fivio Foreign, Sheff G, Smoove'L, Bizzy Banks, 22Gz, and Pop Smoke collaborated with U.K. drill producers like 808Melo, Yamaica Productions, Yoz Beats, Tommyprime, and A.X.L. Beats, and later Brooklyn drill producers like 808Melo, Yamaica Productions, Yoz Beats, Tommyprime, and A.X.L.

Beats.] The song "Welcome to the Party" by Pop Smoke, produced by 808Melo, was a big hit in 2019, with remixes from Nicki Minaj, Meek Mill, and British MC Skepta. Sheff G's "No Suburban" (issued in 2017) and 22Gz's "Suburban" (published in 2016) are attributed with bringing attention to the subsequent Brooklyn drill.

U.K. drill

U.K. drill is a subgenre of drill music and road rap that began in the Brixton neighborhood of South London in 2012. Drill musicians in the United Kingdom frequently rap about violent and hedonistic criminal lifestyles, drawing largely on the Chicago drill music style. Those that make this type of music are usually members of gangs or hail from low-income areas where crime is a way of life for many. Road rap, a British kind of gangster rap that grew popular in the years before the drill, is closely tied to U.K. drill music. U.K. drill is known for its aggressive language and inflammatory lyrics.

Latin trap

Latin trap is a trap music subgenre that started in Puerto Rico. It gained popularity after 2007 and has since spread throughout Latin America. It is a direct descendent of southern hip hop and is influenced by Reggaeton. Latin trap is similar to mainstream trap because it features lyrics about street life.

Characteristics

Latin trap is a type of Latin hip hop that draws inspiration from both Southern hip hop and Puerto Rican genres like Reggaeton and Dembow. While preserving the trap style sonic circuitry, vocals include a blend of rapping and singing, frequently in Spanish. Latin trap lyrics frequently refer to street life, violence, sex, and narcotics.

History

The 2000s

Latin trap began in Puerto Rico and has now spread across Latin America. The precise date of origin is unknown and has been the subject of much discussion. According to Ozuna, a Puerto Rican Reggaeton and Latin trap singer, it began in 2007 with the song "El Pistolón," which was performed by Arcángel& De La Ghetto, Yaga& Mackie, and Jowell& Randy (the former two were duo at the time). De La Ghetto, on the other hand, claims to have been doing Latin trap since 2005 or 2006, when people believed he was "mad." At the time, Reggaeton musicians aimed to expose American hip hop and R&B to a Spanish audience.

The 2010s

Around 2014, musicians like Alvaro Diaz, Myke Towers, and FueteBillete, the first Puerto Rican rappers

THE HISTORY OF TRAP

to use early Latin trap sounds, began posting their tracks on social media channels. This new sound grew in popularity in Puerto Rico, and much Latin trap hits emerged, including Bryant Myers' "Esclava Remix," Lary Over and Brytiago's "T Me Enamoraste Remix," Farruko's "Ella y Yo," and De La Ghetto's "La Ocasión," which Ozuna credits with introducing Latin trap to the rest of the world.

"Rappers and Reggaetoneros from Puerto Rico have incorporated parts of trap–the lurching bass lines, jittering 808s, and the eyes-half-closed atmosphere–into banger after banger," The Fader said in July 2017. In an August 2017 piece for Billboard's "A Brief History Of" series, they sought the help of some of the genre's biggest names, including Ozuna, De La Ghetto, Bad Bunny, Farruko, and Messiah, to tell the story of Latin trap. "[Jorge] Fonseca featured Puerto Rican musicians like Anuel AA, Bryant Myers, and Noriel on the collection Trap Capos: Season 1, which became the first "Latin trap" L.P. to hit number one on Billboard's Latin Rhythm Albums chart," according to Rolling Stone's Elias Leight.

Much additional Reggaeton and Latin trap musicians, such as Bad Bunny, added to the development of the genre, which exploded in popularity. Bad Bunny has collaborated with several well-known American musicians, including Nicki Minaj, Travis Scott, and Cardi B, on various tracks that have charted on Billboard's Hot Latin Songs chart. He quickly rose to prominence as the face of the Latin trap's meteoric increase in popularity.

Bad Bunny was one of the first Latin trap musicians to ever rhyme on the radio, thanks to collaborations with other artists like his performance in Becky G's "Mayores." His performance on the radio has boosted Latin trap's popularity in the United States. In December 2018, he released his debut album X 100pre, which won a Latin Grammy for Best Urban Music Album.

Nio Garcia, Casper Magico, Darell, Ozuna, Bad Bunny, and Nicky Jam released the single "TeBoté" in April 2018, which is a mix of Latin trap and Reggaeton. It was the first song to hit number one on the Billboard Hot Latin Songs chart using Latin trap influences. On YouTube, it has received over 1.8 billion views.

Cardi B's breakthrough single "I Like It," which featured Bad Bunny and J Balvin, became the first Latin trap song to top the Billboard Hot 100 chart of 2018.

Criticism

The lyrics' obscenity and lasciviousness prevent Latin trap from being broadcast on the radio. Maluma's song "Cuatro Babys" has sparked a lot of debate because the lyrics appear to condone direct violence against women. On Change.org, a petition was started calling for the

THE HISTORY OF TRAP

music to be taken down from all digital platforms. Despite the uproar, "Cuatro Babys" has only grown in popularity, with the song going quadruple platinum.

Latin trap has a considerable, but mostly underground, following as a result of this.

Anuel AA released a diss track directed at fellow rapper Cosculluela on September 15, 2018. The song was heavily panned for its profanity and derogatory statements regarding gays and H.I.V. patients. Gazmey's show at the Coliseo de Puerto Rico, slated for October 12 of that year, was postponed by his production team and chief producer, Paco López because of the public outcry. Later, Gazmey apologized for the song.

Phonk

D.J. Screw, X-Raided, Phonk Beta, DJ Squeeky, and the group Three 6 Mafia were among the genre's early pioneers in the 2000s in the Southern United States, primarily in Houston and Memphis. The genre became more modern in the late 2010s because of streaming platforms like SoundCloud and placed a greater emphasis on jazz and classic hip hop, rather than the "gritty, dark, Memphis-oriented sound" of the early phonk.

"Drift phonk" is a subgenre of phonk that arose in Russia, popularized by TikTok and the drift community on social media. Its major traits are the usage of cowbells and high bass. It's commonly seen in Lo-Fi videos of drifting autos.

History

In the mid-1990s, Phonk was inspired by trap roots in the Southern United States. D.J. Screw, X-Raided, Phonk Beta, DJ Squeeky, and the collective Three 6 Mafia all helped lay the groundwork for the genre to develop several years later, with Houston chopped and screwed being regarded as the genre's forerunner. While phonk was popular in the late 2000s, it resurfaced in the early 2010s. Key producers like Space Ghost Purrp and D.J. Smokey took a darker, sinister approach to 1990s trap music.

Space Ghost Purrp popularized the term "phonk" with songs like Pheel Tha Phonk, Bringin' Tha Phonk, and Keep Bringin' Tha Phonk. Ryan Celsius, Trill Phonk, Emotional Tokyo, and uncommon were among the YouTube channels that helped promote the genre. Before the genre achieved genuine traction in the mid-2010s, Phonk producers continued to push this sound underground.

By the end of 2017, Phonk had grown into a more current sound, moving away from the "gritty, dark, Memphis-oriented sound" and including more modern vocalists, as well as bringing more jazz and classic hip hop to the forefront. Ryan Celsius has defined this stream of Phonk as "rare Phonk," with "more of a crisper, more mainstream trap sound." Phonk was one of the most popular genres on SoundCloud between 2016 and 2018, with the hashtag #phonk among the most trending each year.

Characteristics

Phonk is defined by classic Memphis rap voices and samples from early 1990s hip hop and is directly inspired by 1990s Memphis rap. These are frequently used in conjunction with jazz and funk samples. To generate a darker sound, the chopped and screwed approach is primarily applied.

The fact that Phonk is not bound to a regional "scene" is a feature of the genre; this is due to the nature of SoundCloud as an online platform, which emphasizes subgenres developed from hip hop and experimental pop. "What is amazing about [Phonk] is that these artists come from all over the world: you can find producers of Phonk in Canada, the United States, France, and even Russia!" said Phonk artist Lowpocus in a 2017 interview. D.J. Smokey, DJ Yung Vamp, Soudiere, NxxxxxS, and Mythic are among the acts linked with "new-age Phonk."

Aside from its musical feature, Phonk has a distinct look that incorporates cartoon visuals such as Simpson's fan art. For EPs and albums, Phonk musicians frequently use "Pen & Pixel" style artwork.

Subgenres

In Russia, a subgenre of Phonk known as "drift Phonk" appeared in the late 2010s. The usage of heavy bass, cowbells, and distorted sounds distinguish it, and the lyrics of the samples are frequently unrecognizable. Drift Phonk movies frequently incorporate footage of drifting and street racing automobiles, making them popular in the online car culture. The TikTok app helped the genre gain popularity quickly. Kaito Shoma, Pharmacist, and Lxst Cxntury, all Russian makers, are among the most well-known.

FUSION TRAP AND ITS GENRES

E.D.M. Trap

Trap, often known as E.D.M. trap, is a piece of electronic dance music (E.D.M.) genre that emerged in the early 2010s. It combines trap music, a subgenre of Southern hip hop, with E.D.M. characteristics such as build-ups, drops, and breakdowns. Trap's transition into pop and E.D.M. was aided by several artists.

History

Trap music was merged into a kind of electronic dance music (E.D.M.) in 2012, resulting in "dirty, violent beats, gloomy melodies." Electronic music musicians such as T.N.G.H.T., Baauer, RL Grime, and Flosstradamus boosted trap's popularity and brought it to a wider audience. Techno, dub, and electro sounds were blended with Roland TR-808 drum samples and vocal samples to create this genre.

These different trap offshoots were increasingly popular in the latter half of 2012 and had a major impact on the American electronic dance music industry. Producers and fans initially referred to the music simply as "trap," which led to confusion among fans of both rappers and electronic producers when the term "trap" was referred to both rappers and electronic producers' music.

Instead of referring to a single genre, the term "trap" refers to two distinct hip hop and dance music subgenres. Some have dubbed the latest wave of the genre "E.D.M. trap" to distinguish it from the rap genre. Producers frequently use the terms "trap-techno" and "trap step" to describe the musical structure of a single track. Incorporation and artistic influences from dubstep have been apparent in the emerging E.D.M. trap, with trap being touted as the succeeding phase of dubstep in the mid-2010s. The new phase, which has been rising in prominence since 2013, often plays at 140 BPM with heavy bass drops.

In 2013, a fan-made video of electronic trap artist Baauer's single, "Harlem Shake" by Filthy Frank (also known as Joji) became an internet craze, propelling the track to become the first trap song to reach number one

THE HISTORY OF TRAP

on the Billboard Hot 100. This challenge entailed one person dancing to the beat of the song until the beat dropped, at which point everyone else in the video would join in with the person dancing at the start. DJ Craze, Baauer, and Flosstradamus were among the five E.D.M. trap producers who played at the 2013 Ultra Music Festival in the United States. A "trap stage" was presented during the 2013 Tomorrowland festival.

All Trap Music released their inaugural compilation album on February 10, 2013, featuring 19 tracks from artists such as RL Grime, Flosstradamus, Baauer, Bro Safari, and 12th Planet. The music press dubbed it "the world's biggest-selling E.D.M. trap album ever," and it reached number two on the iTunes dance list. Vibe called it "the world's biggest-selling E.D.M. trap album ever." D.J. Snake and Lil Jon released the single "Turn Down for What" in 2013, which was a financial and critical success in various countries.

"The year's nutsiest party jam was also the ultimate protest banger for a generation fed up with everything," says Rolling Stone magazine of "Turn Down for What." "Lil Jon offers the dragon-fire yell for a hilarious, wonderful, glow stick-punk fuck you, while D.J. Snake brings the synapse-rattling E.D.M. and Southern trap music."

Trap music has gained popularity around the world, particularly in South Korea. The K-pop pair G-Dragon and Taeyang of the South Korean boy band B.I.G.B.A.N.G. released their single "Good Boy" in November 2014, which had a significant trap and electronic elements. The song received excellent reviews from music reviewers and received 2 million views in less than 24 hours. When B.I.G.B.A.N.G. released their commercial success single "Bang, Bang, Bang" in June 2015, the trap returned to the K-pop arena once more. In South Korea, the single was a critical and economic triumph, hitting the top of the Gaon Digital Chart and selling over 1 million digital singles by August 2015.

When Philadelphia production trio, *Working on Dying* recorded Eternal Atake, Francisville rapper Lil Uzi Vert's third studio album, in the late 2010s, trap mixed with synth-pop and emo-pop. Working on Dying's Brandon Finessin got eight producer credits on Lil Uzi Vert's emo-rap album, which included hyper pop and E.D.M. elements alongside traditional trap drum sequences. As a result, Lil Uzi Vert and Brandon Finessin topped the Producers and Songwriters Top 100s on the Billboard charts together. Working on Dying's electronic approach to trap music spawned an offshoot scene of hyper pop trap beats from obscure YouTube producers.

In the late 2010s, a new style of trap music known as trap wave (or hardwave) arose, fusing trap music with synth-wave.

Rap metal

Rap metal is a rap-rock and alternative metal subgenre that blends hip hop and heavy metal. Heavy metal guitar riffs, funk metal components, rapped vocals, and turntables are combined.

History

Origins and early development (the 1980s–early 1990s)

Anthrax (pictured) is regarded as one of the pioneers of rap metal with the publication of its extended disc I'm the Man.

Rap metal evolved from rap-rock, music that combined hip hop vocal and instrumental elements with rock. The genre's origins may be traced back to hip-hop artists like Beastie Boys, MC Strecker, Cypress Hill, Esham, and Run-DMC sampling heavy metal songs, as well as rock bands like 24-7 Spyz and Faith No More fusing heavy metal and hip hop influences.

Rage Against the Machine, according to Scott Ian of Anthrax, founded it. However, before Rage Against the Machine, Urban Dance Squad (founded in 1986) merged rap and metal, though Rage Against the Machine is credited with refining the sound, giving rap-rock an edginess and grit that would define the genre for years to come.

For their extended play *I'm the Man,* released in 1987, the heavy metal band Anthrax blended hip hop and heavy metal. The following year, for his 1988 single "Iron Man," from his first album Swass, rapper Sir Mix-a-Lot teamed up with Metal Church, loosely based on the Black Sabbath song of the same name.

Rap metal can be heard on the tune "Test" from the industrial metal band Ministry's 1989 album The Mind Is a Terrible Thing to Taste, which featured rappers The Grand Wizard (K. Lite) and The Slogan God (Tommie Boyskee) on vocals.

Legendary West Coast Rapper, Ice-T established a heavy metal band named Body Count in 1990 and performed a set that was half rap songs and half metal songs at the 1991 Lollapalooza festival. Another two pioneers of the genre are Stuck Mojo and Clawfinger, both of whom were established in 1989. In 1991, Anthrax teamed up with Public Enemy for a hip hop/thrash metal rendition of the latter's "Bring the Noise." Tourniquet collaborated with the hip hop group P.I.D. on the song "Spineless" off their album Psycho Surgery in 1991.

THE HISTORY OF TRAP

The rise in popularity (the 1990s–early 2000s)

Rap metal became a prominent genre of music in the 1990s. The song "Epic" by Faith No More, for example, was a huge hit and reached number 9 on the Billboard Hot 100. The Judgment Night soundtrack was released in 1993, and it contained various collaborations with rappers, musicians, and rock and metal bands.

Rage Against the Machine's debut album, Evil Empire, debuted at number one on the Billboard 200 in 1996, and their third studio album, The Battle of Los Angeles, debuted at number one in 1999, selling 430,000 copies in its first week. Each of the band's albums was certified platinum. Biohazard shared the stage with Ozzy Osbourne, Slayer, Danzig, Fear Factory, and Sepultura at Ozzfest. Biohazard went on a short European co-headlining tour with Suicidal Tendencies to promote the album.

On August 18, 1998, Atlantic released Kid Rock's Devil Without a Cause, which included the single "Welcome 2 the Party (Ode 2 the Old School)," and Kid Rock supported the album by performing on the Vans Warped Tour. Although the 1998 Warped Tour in Northampton, Massachusetts, sparked regional interest in Massachusetts and New England, sales of "Welcome 2 The Party" and "Devil Without a Cause" were modest. The single "I Am The Bullgod" had a lot of exposure during the summer and fall of 1998 on Massachusetts rock stations W.Z.L.X. and WAAF.

He met and became friends with MTV broadcaster Carson Daly while DJing at a party in early December 1998. He persuaded Daly to secure him a spot on MTV, and on December 28, 1998, he performed on MTV Fashionably Loud in Miami, Florida, causing a stir and even upstaging Jay-Z. With the release of his third song, "Bawitdaba," in May, his sales took up, and by April 1999, Devil Without a Cause had gained gold status.

The Devil went platinum the next month, just as he prophesied. Kid Rock's first major tour, Limptropolis, featured Staind as an opener for Limp Bizkit. With a performance at Woodstock in 1999, he cemented his superstar status, and on July 24, 1999, he was certified double platinum. The next single, "Cowboy," a combination of southern rock, country, and rap, was even more successful, reaching the Top 40. It even became Jeff Jarrett's theme song on W.C.W. The slow back porch blues ballad "Only God Knows Why," rock's following single, was the album's biggest hit, peaking at No. 19 on the Billboard Hot 100.

It was one of the first tracks to incorporate autotune. The album had sold 7 million copies by the time the final single, "Wasting Time," was released. On April 17, 2003, the R.I.A.A. certified Devil Without a Cause as 11 times platinum. Actual sales in 2013 were 9.3 million, according to Nielsen SoundScan. At the 2000 Grammy Awards, Kid Rock was nominated for Best New Artist, but Christina Aguilera won.

He was nominated for Best Hard Rock Performance for "Bawitdaba," but Metallica's "Whiskey in the Jar" won. Ice Cube's long-awaited album War & Peace Vol. 1 (The War Disc) was published in 1998, and it featured nu-metal and rap metal influences on some tracks. The album debuted at No. 7 on the Billboard 200 list in its first week, selling 180,000 copies.

It peaked in popularity during the summer of 1999, with the Port Huron Times-Herald describing it as a "bipolar buffet of brutal rap-metal and mushy teen pop." Around this time, the style received popular criticism, especially following the tumultuous Woodstock 1999 festival, which featured several musicians linked with rap metal and nu/alternative metal, including Kid Rock, Limp Bizkit, Rage Against the Machine, and Reveille.

Jeff Brogowski, a pop-punk artist, told The Morning Call newspaper in 1999 that "These macho rap-metal bands are incredibly cruel. Take a look at what occurred at Woodstock (last summer). All the looting, bloodshed, and burning. There's something unusual going on. Perhaps it has something to do with the recent economic boom. It's starting to resemble the

'80s when so many people and bands were so arrogant."

Significant Other, the 1999 album by the nu/rap metal band Limp Bizkit, debuted at No. 1 on the Billboard 200, selling 643,874 copies in its first week. The album sold an extra 335,000 copies in its second week of the sale. Chocolate Starfish and the Hot Dog Flavored Water, the band's follow-up album, set a record for highest week-one sales of a rock album, selling over one million copies in the United States in its first week of release, with 400,000 of those sales coming on the first day, making it the fastest-selling rock album ever, breaking Pearl Jam's Vs.

In infest, Papa Roach's major-label debut became platinum smash the same year. Cypress Hill's Skull & Bones, released in 2000, included six tracks on which rappers B-Real and Sen Dog were backed by a band that included Fear Factory members Christian Olde Wolbers and Dino Cazares, as well as Rage Against the Machine drummer Brad Wilk. With Wolbers, Fear Factory drummer Raymond Herrera, and Deftones guitarist Stephen Carpenter, B-Real founded Kush, a rap-metal band. Kush is more violent than other bands in the genre, according to B-Real. Sen Dog founded

SX-10 in 1996, and the group performs rap rock and rap metal.

The Fundamental Elements of Southtown, a 1999 album by the rap-metal band P.O.D., earned platinum in 2000 and was the 143rd best-selling album of the year. Linkin Park's debut album, Hybrid Theory, was released in late 2000, and it is still the best-selling debut album of any act in the twenty-first century, as well as the best-selling nu-metal album of all time.

The album was also the best-selling album of all genres in 2001, outselling popular pop acts such as Backstreet Boys and N'Sync. The band won a Grammy Award for their second single, "Crawling," and their fourth single, "In the end," was released late in 2001 and became one of the most well-known songs of the first decade of the twenty-first century. Crazy Town, a rap-rock band, burst into the popular success of nu-metal with their 1999 album The Gift of Game, particularly with their number one hit single "Butterfly," which peaked at number one on multiple charts, including the Billboard Hot 100, in March 2001 and stayed there for 23 weeks.

It also reached No. 1 on the Modern Rock Tracks and Hot Dance Singles charts, as well as No. 6 on the Rhythmic Top 40, No. 2 on the Top 40 Mainstream list, and No. 4 on the Top 40 Tracks charts. On the Billboard 200, their album The Gift of Game reached number nine. The album sold over 2.5 million copies worldwide, with over 1.5 million in the United States alone. Saliva's Every Six Seconds, released the same year, was a commercial triumph, debuting at No. 6 on the Billboard 200. Satellite, a 2001 album by P.O.D., went triple platinum and reached #6 on the Billboard 200 chart.

Trap metal

Trap metal (also known as rage core, death rap, industrial trap, and scream rap) is a fusion genre that incorporates trap music, heavy metal, and other genres such as industrial and nu-metal. Distorted beats, hip hop, flows, harsh voices, and down-tuned heavy metal guitars are all hallmarks of the genre. Kerrang! Cites Bones is one of the genre's pioneers, claiming that the band began performing trap metal compositions around 2014.

Scarlxrd, a British rapper who is widely regarded as a pioneer of trap metal, is commonly connected with the genre. O.G. Maco's 2014 eponymous E.P., according to W.Q.H.T., was a component of the genre's early growth. Dropout Kings, Bone Crew, Ghostemane, ZillaKami, Fever 333, Ho99o9, City Morgue, Kid Bookie, Rico Nasty, Kim Dracula, and $uicideboy$ are among the musicians linked with trap metal, as are the early careers of XXXTentacion, 6ix9ine, and Ski Mask the Slump God.

Hardcore punk influences some musicians like Ho99o9, ZillaKami, and 6ix9ine, whereas Ghostemane's music incorporates elements of black metal, gothic rock, and emo.

Country trap

The "country trap" hit "Old Town Road" by 20-year-old rapper Lil Nas X attained massive international popularity in 2019. The song smashed many U.S. streaming records and charted at number one on the Billboard Hot 100 for a record nineteen weeks, thanks to several following versions, including a remix featuring country singer Billy Ray Cyrus. Blanco Brown's "The Git Up" is also described as a "trap-country" song by the U.S.A. Today, became viral in June 2019. Other prominent country trap songs include Lil Nas X and Cardi B's "Rodeo" and R.M.R.'s "Rascal."

Collaborations

A harmonica is featured on the Mo Thugs Family hit "Ghetto Cowboy" (1998). "Cruise (Remix)" (2012) by Florida Georgia Line featuring Nelly "ushered in the tide of escapist dreams set to syncopated drum loops that became known as 'bro-country," according to Rolling Stone. Nelly's portion "just connected," according to Florida Georgia Line, enabling the "Cruise" remix to reach No. 1 and No. 4 on the Billboard Hot Country Songs and Hot 100 charts, respectively. It also became the first country hit to receive R.I.A.A. diamond certification.

"Both of Us" was written by B.o.B and Taylor Swift, a country artist (2012). Swift's country vocals are mixed with hip-hop and banjos on the single. It reached the top 10 in Australia and New Zealand and the top 20 in the United States.

The controversial song "Accidental Racist" was recorded by country singer Brad Paisley and rapper L.L. Cool J for Paisley's 2013 album Wheelhouse.

Other collaborations include Nappy Roots' "Po' Folks" (2002) with Anthony Hamilton, Bubba Sparxxx's "Country Folks" (2012) with Colt Ford and Danny Boone, Jason Aldean and Ludacris' "Dirt Road Anthem" (remix), and Meghan Linsey's "Try Harder Than That" with Bubba Sparxxx (2014).

Popularity

Physical album sales of country rap albums are greater in more rural locations, where fans do not have access to the Internet to stream or download music. There are various country rap festivals where performers perform for crowds of up to 7,000 people.

Politics

Some southern artists decry the name "hick-hop," as Struggle Jennings put it: "I love the country, I love the South, I've been fishing and hunting, but I'm not a hick. I'm not hick-hop." Because of some right-leaning politics voiced by artists like Upchurch and Forgiato Blow, country rap artists' political philosophy is looked at as being right-wing or conservative; however, the political ideology of country rap artists spans the complete spectrum of political opinions.

NOTABLE TRAP ALBUMS TO DATE

Some claim that Waka Flocka Flame's famous Flockaveli album in 2010 was the beginning of the modern trap sound and that everything released prior to 2010 impacted that sound but was not truly trap as we know it now. So, even though some of the pre-2010 albums on this list aren't technically trapped records, we included them nevertheless — either because they're Southern classics that affected trap's direction or just because we think these are the best albums by artists that are frequently labeled as trap artists (even if their best albums arguably are not strictly trap-music).

T.I. – Trap Muzik (2003)

T.I.'s Trap Muzik is his second studio album, and it's a significant improvement from his lackluster debut. I'm Serious (2001). Trap Muzik is a Southern classic, a completely gratifying front-to-back listening experience with plenty of intensity and personality. This seminal album features trap music in one of its earlier incarnations, serving as a reminder of how long the sub-genre existed before exploding in the early to mid-2010s. Trap Muzik is an essential record in the context of trap and Southern rap because it helped birth the genre.

Young Jeezy - Let's Get It: Thug Motivation 101 (2005)

While artists like T.I., Yo Gotti, and Gucci Mane helped pioneer trap in the early 2000s, Atlanta rapper Young Jeezy helped expand the genre and push it to the next level. Let's Get It: Thug Motivation 101, his Def Jam debut, included nearly eighty minutes of early trap music at its best. The bounce and crunk-flavored rhythms Young Jeezy worked with are what made this album a (pre)trap classic. Let's Get It: Thug Motivation 101 was a landmark album for the artist, and it remains his best effort to this day.

T.I. - King (2006)

With a strong blend of radio club and street tracks, T.I.'s fourth studio album, King, is his greatest and most consistent record to date. This album marks the pinnacle of T.I.'s discography, with award-winning production and T.I. at the peak of his game. King comes close to living up to its own hyperbole and would have if a few filler tracks amid the very long 70-minute tracklist had been removed. Even if King is about 15 minutes overlong, this is unquestionably a Southern masterpiece.

Lil Wayne - Tha Carter III (2008)

Pop-rap with trap influences. Tha Carter III is Lil Wayne's sixth studio album, following Tha Carter II and a long string of mixtape releases and guest appearances on other Hip Hop and R&B artists' records, all of which helped to increase Lil Wayne's mainstream exposure, which was further aided by features on this album from high-profile artists like Jay-Z, T-Pain, Busta Rhymes, and Kanye West, among others.

Even if Lil Wayne isn't a trapper, it's not a leap to say he helped birth the mumble trap genre, which has spawned a legion of face-tatted Lil Clones who have been filling the mainstream with a never-ending stream of generic braindead music.

The Carter III is one of the most important albums of the aughts. The album's back half is substantially weaker than its first, but iconic Lil Wayne bangers like "A Milli," "Dr. Carter," and "Let The Beat Build" make up for it. This isn't technically a trap album, but we believe it contributed to the genre's development (no Young Thug without Lil Wayne) and so deserves to be included on this list.

T.I. - Paper Trail (2008)

T.I.'s sixth studio album, Paper Trail, was released when he was at the peak of his career. T.I.'s third-best album, Paper Trail, is his biggest commercial success. There's a lot of mainstream appeals here, as well as pre-trap sensibilities.

Gucci Mane - The State vs. Radric Davis (2009)

Gucci Mane is one of the godfathers of the trap genre, and he has one of the most lengthy discographies in all of (t)rap music, with a never-ending stream of mixtapes and albums. Gucci Mane is certainly a quantity over quality artist (like trap Kool Keith), but there isn't much noteworthy music among the dozens of projects he's released since his recording debut in 2005.

Despite a few filler tracks and several bad interludes/skits, The State vs. the People is his sixth studio album. Radric Davis is likely his strongest overall endeavor (out of the more than six dozen mixtapes he's made).

Waka Flocka Flame - Flockavelli (2010)

Everything that came before Flockavelli may be classified as pre-trap, and we can classify everything that has come after as post-trap. Perhaps exaggerating Flockavelli's importance, but the reality remains that this was a very substantial album–a game-changer that laid the framework for the next generation of trappers. Waka Flocka Flame's contagious energy and personality propels him to that next level. This trapped classic is a huge album comprising of bangers that are aging incredibly nicely, with bombastic bass-heavy beats, crisp synths, and aggressive rapping.

A$AP Ferg - Trap Lord (2013)

A$AP Ferg, a major member of the A$ A.P. Mob collective, releases his debut studio album, Trap Lord. A$AP Rocky, Bone Thugs-n-Harmony, French Montana, Trinidad James, Schoolboy Q, Waka Flocka Flame, Aston Matthews, B-Real, and Onyx make guest appearances on the album, which helped make it a success.

There are plenty of bangers on Trap Lord, including "Let It Go," "Shabba," "Lord," "Hood Pope," "Fergivicious," "Dump Dump," "Didn't Wanna Do That," "Murda Something," "Make A Scene," "Fuck Out My Face," and "Cocaine Castle." This is an A$ A.P. Mob album. By far, it's Ferg's strongest work and Trap Lord is a charismatic and energetic record with deliciously dark and gothic production.

Future - Monster (2014)

After DS2, Monster is Future's best project. Monster's most appealing feature is its dark and atmospheric production, which is entirely because of Metro Boomin, whose imprint can be found all over this tape.

Young Thug - Barter 6 (2015)

Young Thug is one of his generation's most significant figures, with his music influencing the present trap sound. Thugger, who is known for his quirky singing style and attire, began his career by releasing a series of indie mixtapes, starting with *I Came from Nothing* in 2011.

He signed with Gucci Mane's 1017 Records in early 2013, and later that year, he released *1017 Thug*, his label debut mixtape, to widespread acclaim. Since his chart debut with the track "Stoner" in 2014, Young Thug has been one of the most distinctive and polarizing contemporary rap artists, violating Hip Hop traditions while defying gender and sexuality preconceptions.

Young Thug's lyrics are sometimes serious, sometimes just amusing, more often over-the-top or completely ludicrous–it doesn't matter; you don't listen to him for lyrical depth; you listen to him for his melodic mumble flows. His extravagance and intensity are palpable, and he understands how to make trap music exciting and contagious without relying entirely on production. The tape is well-produced and polished, and the deep 808 bounces do the job. Young Thug's first major project,

Barter 6, launched him on the route to becoming the most important trap musician of the decade.

Travis Scott - Rodeo (2015)

After his first two mixtapes, Owl Pharaoh and Days Before Rodeo, Houston rapper Travis Scott finally releases his long-awaited debut album, Rodeo. Quavo, Future, 2 Chainz, Juicy J, Kacy Hill, The Weeknd, Swae Lee, Chief Keef, Kanye West, Justin Bieber, Young Thug, Toro y Moi, and Schoolboy Q all make appearances on the album, which was produced by Travis Scott alongside several high-profile producers including WondaGurl, Allen Ritter, Mike Dean, Metro Boomin, Frank Dukes, and Sonny Digital.

Rodeo is unique, daring in its experimentation and unlike anything else heard before (or subsequently) in the trap genre, which is rife with genericity. Rodeo's futuristic and psychedelic vibes are enthralling, the dark and artsy production is fantastic, and most of the vocal contributions blend seamlessly with the musical backdrops. Travis Scott is also one of the few musicians who can use autotune as an instrument rather than a means of masking a lack of skill.

Rodeo paved the path for Travis Scott to become one of rap's top paid artists. This album is for the old heads who remain anti-trap and other Hip Hop diehards who

THE HISTORY OF TRAP

are willing to move out of their comfort zones and give the genre a shot.

Future - DS2 (2015)

Future's third studio album, DS2, is his best overall work. His lyrics are forgettable, but it's his swagger that propels this album along - along with the album's dark production. Metro Boomin, who always manages to place his instantly recognized imprint on each beat he creates–something like a trap D.J. Premier–is largely responsible for the trippy beats on DS2.

"Thought It Was A Drought," "I Serve The Base," "Where Ya At," "Slave Master," "Colossal," "Stick Talk," "Blood On The Money," "The Percocet & Stripper Joint," and "F**k Up Some Commas" are just a few of the outstanding tracks on DS2. This is a classic trap album.

Young Thug - Jeffery (2016)

Young Thug's best tape since Barter 6 and perhaps his best overall effort to date is Jeffery. The Slime Season series, which came after Barter 6 and before Jeffrey, was good, but Young Thug outdid himself with this tape. Thugger's experiments with varied vocal inflections work out brilliantly — his voice is like an instrument here, an intrinsic component of the impeccably constructed beats and synths. The lyrical material is nonsensical, deliberately silly, and ludicrous - but you don't listen to a Young Thug disc for deep lyrical insights; you listen to it to chill out.

Denzel Curry - Imperial (2016)

Denzel Curry's second studio album isn't quite a trap record, but it includes enough trap elements to make this list. Imperial is a fantastic album that is underappreciated in Denzel Curry's discography. This is a slam dunk.

Sybyr - Anti-World (2016)

Sybyr (a.k.a. Syringe) collaborated with Anti-World on an intriguing initiative. On Anti-World, Sybyr takes a fresh approach, skewing trap-genre tropes. Call it experimental, call it edgy, call it whatever you want. This is an angsty downhill spiral that gets you by the throat and won't let go. Aggressive raps with distorted, noise-laced trap beats: this is an angsty downward spiral that grabs you by the neck and won't let go. Rough around the edges, with a few errors (for example, the horrible ego Mackey function on "Raging"), but this underappreciated effort is FIRE.

Migos - Culture (2017)

There's a lot to detest about Migos, and it's all on display here. The jerky flows, irritating ad-libs, and excessive use of autotune, as well as the self-aggrandizing, misogynistic, and stupid lyrics. Despite the Migos'

THE HISTORY OF TRAP

issues, culture remains a satisfying experience. Culture is simple and dumb fun, notable if only for "Bad And Boujee" (feat. Lil Uzi Vert), which is a classic track, of course. The instrumentals are banging, and the songs are engaging and catchy. This is Migos' best album in my opinion.

2 Chainz - Pretty Girls Like Trap Music (2017)

Pretty Girls Like Trap Music is 2 Chainz's most influential album to date. FKi, Honorable C.N.O.T.E., Mike Dean, Mike Will Made-It, and Murda Beatz, among others, contributed to the album's production. Gucci Mane, Quavo, Travis Scott, Nicki Minaj, Swae Lee, Drake, Ty Dolla Sign, Trey Songz, Jhené Aiko, Pharrell, and Monica all make appearances as well. The features, as well as the production, are all exceptional. The singles "Good Drank," "It's A Vibe," and "4 AM" are obvious features, but Pretty Girls Like Trap Music's appeal lies in its harmony. One of the few trap albums with longevity.

Denzel Curry - TA13OO (2018)

Denzel Curry's magnum opus, TA13OO, is one of our favorites on this list. This album is chock-full of psychedelic bangers, with an atmospheric production that is hard-hitting and unpredictable, delivering the mayhem required to match Denzel Curry's ferocious flows. It's debatable whether the album's three-act notion of getting "darker" as the tracks advance actually works, but it doesn't really matter because TA1300 is a typical trap masterpiece.

PlayboiCarti - Die Lit (2018)

This is an album that we should absolutely despise. Playboi Carti is the worst kind of mumble rapper, and Die Lit's lyrical material is utter nonsense. However, despite (or perhaps because of) its foolishness, this record has an inexplicable attraction; for some reason, this album is F.U.N. Die Lit's deep-bass beats accomplish the job, and Playboi Carti's rhymes don't offend but give the perfect taste to the instrumentals — something to do with personality and style, I'm sure. It's difficult to confess, but this project is a guilty pleasure of mine. It's okay to switch off your brain now and then, and Die Lit is the perfect album to do so too.

Metro Boomin - Not All Heroes Wear Capes (2018)

Metro Boomin, an Atlanta-based producer, is our favorite trap producer, and Not All Heroes Wear Capes is his debut studio album. A producer's album is usually always a mixed bag because not all the vocalists enlisted can be counted on to deliver, and Not All Heroes Wear Capes is no exception. Gucci Mane, Travis Scott, 21 Savage, Gunna, Young Thug, J. Balvin, Offset, Kodak Black, Wizkid, Swae Lee, and Drake all make appearances. The album would have been stronger without the last three's contributions, but Not All Heroes Wear Capes is an engrossing and immensely fun listen even if it lacks Metro Boomin's darkest and hardest-hitting beats.

Travis Scott - ASTROWORLD (2018)

ASTROWORLD is another Travis Scott winner, a step up from his relatively dismal second album Birds In The Trap Sing McKnight (2016). Travis Scott sounds fresh again on ASTROWORLD, proving that he is one of the few artists who can get away with autotune crooning–a lot of artists use the autotune to hide the fact that they can't rap, but Travis Scott is clearly talented enough that he doesn't need it. ASTROWORLD is the pinnacle of the psychedelic trap.

21 Savage - I Am > I Was (2018)

I Am > I Was (pronounced "I am greater than I was") is 21 Savage's second solo studio album, following Issa Album (2017) and the excellent Without Warning collaboration with Offset and Metro Boomin – a project that would have made this list if it had been a little longer than the EP-like 33 minutes it lasts. I Am > I Was is probably 21 Savage's strongest and most well-rounded album to date, even if his 2020 collaboration with Metro Boomin, Savage Mode II, comes close.

I Am > I Was is a mature project with excellent hooks and production — the album's tracks have enough variation to keep things interesting and avoid feeling like any other bland, standard trap album. While J. Cole, Offset, Gunna, Lil Baby, Schoolboy Q, and Childish Gambino (among others) all contribute vocals to I Am > I Was, 21 Savage actually doesn't need many guests to spice up his albums - his flow is slick enough to carry an album on its own. There are a few filler tracks generally and this is a strong effort from one of trap's most promising artists.

Future of Trap Music

"All these rappers are all my offspring," Gucci Mane wisely says. Gucci Mane, fresh out of prison, released "All My Children" as the first single from his upcoming album "Everybody Looking" in 2016. He acknowledges the altered rap landscape since his conviction in the song. He brags about his ability to shape the sound of mainstream music. His charisma and hard-hitting southern-style sounds swept the music industry, with a slew of artists adopting his sound. Future, Waka Flocka Flame, Migos, Young Thug, Travi$ Scott, and Fetty Wap were all instrumental in propelling Gucci's sound into the 2010s and establishing Atlanta as the center of trap music.

These few musicians have since influenced a new generation of trap artists who have taken the sound to new places. Lil Yachty applies his pop-friendly demeanor and carefree youthful attitude to his trap songs, crafting his own version of the heavily saturated trap sound. Lil Uzi Vert, a Philadelphia native like myself, is integrating his own gothic and moody attitude into the conventional trap approach. While these musicians have pushed the sound and culture in new areas, weird and outlier trap acts have emerged because of their efforts.

Lil Pump and Lil Xan could be the symbols of what one considers by the meaning of *degradation trap,* but it is what it is.

AFTERWORD

Trap music has become ingrained in popular society, with a slew of different musicians repeating and churning it out. Trap music evolved from being an honest means of presenting the rags-to-riches story (21 Savage is a good example) to becoming an accessory for white pop musicians in a matter of years. Camila Cabello's summer smash Havana (Ft. Young Thug) is an example of this, as it is simply a Latin-flavored pop tune with an entirely unneeded appearance from Jeffrey himself.

Liam Payne of One Direction fame, for example, has used Quavo as a commodity to make his pop song more accessible to a wider population. This practice of using hip hop musicians (particularly Black artists) as commodities for pop audiences isn't new, but trap music is swiftly sliding into it. As more artists sell their souls for popular culture success, trap music's authenticity is gradually eroding. However, this leaves trap music's future uncertain.

Currently, I believe trap music will take one of two paths. The first is that it will mature as a genre and extend broadly. If we look at the Metal genre, it only lasted a brief time in the mainstream, but it hasn't died as a genre because it has so many diverse versions (Thrash metal, Black Metal, Death Metal, etc.).

New up-and-comers such as Valee, Yung Bans, and Sah Babii all take the trap sound and give it their own spin. If this trend continues, various trap music sub-genres will materialize (Post-Trap, Alternative Trap, for example).

Let's not forget that white, Asian, Latino, Arab and other non-black artists have embraced the trap sound in recent years, thus gaining popularity and spreading the word of hip hop to those who don't know.

Ultimately, it's up to trap musicians and their audiences to save it from becoming another fad, which will be its likely outcome as it materializes further mainstream.

IF YOU DIDN'T KNOW

THE GOLDEN AGE

Hip Hop's "golden age" (or "golden era") is a name given to a period in mainstream Hip Hop—usually cited as between the mid-1980s and the mid-1990s—said to be characterized by its diversity, quality, innovation, and influence. There were strong themes of Afrocentricity and political militancy, while the music was experimental and the sampling, eclectic. There was often a strong jazz influence. The artists most often associated with the phrase are Public Enemy, Boogie Down Productions, Eric B. & Rakim, De La Soul, A Tribe Called Quest, Gang Starr, Big Daddy Kane and the Jungle Brothers.

The golden age is noted for its innovation – a time "when it seemed that every new single reinvented the genre" according to Rolling Stone. Referring to "hip-hop in its golden age", Spin's editor-in-chief Sia Michel says, "there were so many important, groundbreaking albums coming out right about that time", and MTV's Sway Calloway adds: "The thing that made that era so great is that nothing was contrived. Everything was still being discovered and everything was still innovative and new". Writer William Jelani Cobb says "what made the era they inaugurated worthy of the term golden was the sheer number of stylistic innovations that came into existence... in these golden years, a critical mass of mic prodigies were literally creating themselves and their art form at the same time".

The specific time period that the golden age covers varies slightly from different sources. Some place it square in the 1980s to the 1990s. Rolling Stone refers to "rap's '86-'99 Golden Age", and while MSNBC states, "the "Golden Age" of Hip-Hop music: The '80s" and '90s."

WORLD HIP HOP

In Haiti, Hip-Hop was developed in the early 1980s, and is mostly accredited to Master Dji and his songs "Vakans" and "Politik Pam". What later became known as "Rap Kreyòl" grew in popularity in the late 1990s with King Posse and Original Rap Stuff. Due to cheaper recording technology and flows of equipment to Haiti, more Rap Kreyòl groups are recording songs, even after the January 12th earthquake.

In the Dominican Republic, a recording by Santi Y Sus Duendes and Lisa M became the first single of meren-rap, a fusion of Hip Hop and merengue.

New York City experienced a heavy Jamaican hip-hop influence during the 1990s. This influence was brought on by cultural shifts particularly because of the heightened immigration of Jamaicans to New York City and the American-born Jamaican youth who were coming of age during the 1990s. Rap artists such as De La Soul and Black Star have produced albums influenced by Jamaican roots.

In Europe, Africa, and Asia, Hip-Hop began to move from the underground to mainstream audiences and was the domain of both ethnic nationals and immigrants. British hip hop, for example, became a genre of its own and spawned many artists such as Wiley, Dizzee Rascal, The Streets and many more.

Germany produced the well-known "Die Fantastischen Vier" as well as several Turkish performers like the controversial Cartel, Kool Savaş, and Azad. Similarly, France has produced a number of native-born stars, MC Solaar, Rohff, Rim'K or Booba. In the Netherlands, important nineties rappers include The Osdorp Posse, a crew from Amsterdam, Extince, from Oosterhout, and Postmen.

Italy found its own rappers, including Jovanotti, and Articolo, grow nationally renowned, while the Polish scene began in earnest early in the decade with the rise of PM Cool Lee.

In Romania, B.U.G. Mafia came out of Bucharest's Pantelimon neighborhood, and their brand of gangsta rap underlines the parallels between life in Romania's

Communist-era apartment blocks and the housing projects of America's ghettos.

Israel and Palestinian Hip Hop grew greatly in popularity at the end of the decade, with several stars including Palestinian rapper (Tamer Nafer) and Israeli (Subliminal) hitting the scenes.

In Asia, mainstream stars rose to prominence in the Philippines, led by Francis Magalona, Rap Asia, MC Lara and Lady Diane. In Japan, where underground rappers had previously found a limited audience, and popular teen idols brought a style called J-rap to the top of the charts in the middle of the 1990s.

Latinos had played an integral role in the early development of hip hop, and the style had spread to parts of Latin America, such as Cuba, early in its history. In Mexico, popular hip hop began with the success of Calo [disambiguation needed] in the early 1990s. Later in the decade, Hispanic rap groups like Cypress Hill gained fame on the American music charts while Mexican rap rock groups, such as Control Machete, rose to prominence in their country. An annual Cuban Hip Hop concert held at Alamar in Havana helped popularize Cuban hip hop, beginning in 1995. Hip Hop grew steadily more popular in Cuba, mainly because of official governmental support for all musicians.

THE HISTORY OF TRAP

The Brazilian hip hop scene is considered to be the second biggest in the world, just behind American Hip Hop. It is heavily associated with racial and economic inequalities in the country, where a lot of blacks live in impoverished situations in the violent slums, known in Brazil as favelas. São Paulo is where hip hop began in the country, but it soon spread all over Brazil, and today, almost every big Brazilian city, such as Rio de Janeiro, Salvador, Curitiba, Porto Alegre, Belo Horizonte, Recife, and Brasilia, has a hip hop scene.

Racionais MC's, MV Bill, Marcelo D2, Rappin Hood, Jay Nano, Thaíde and Dj Hum, Bonde do Tigrão, Bonde do Rolê, GOG, RZO are considered the most powerful names in Brazilian hip hop music industry.

ACROSS THE WORLD

The continuation of hip hop can also be seen in different national contexts. In Tanzania, maintained popular acts of their own in the early 2000s, infusing local styles of Afrobeat and arabesque melodies, dancehall and hip-hop beats, and Swahili lyrics. Scandinavian, especially Danish and Swedish, performers became well known outside of their country, while Hip Hop continued its spread into new regions, including Russia, Japan, Philippines, Canada, China, Korea, India and especially Vietnam. Of particular importance is the influence on East Asian nations, where hip hop music has become fused with local popular music to form different styles such as K-pop, C-pop, and J-pop.

In the Netherlands, MC Brainpower went from being an underground battle rapper to mainstream recognition in

THE HISTORY OF TRAP

the Benelux, thus influencing numerous rap artists in the region. In Israel, rapper Subliminal reaches out to Israeli youth with political and religious-themed lyrics, usually with a Zionist message. One of the countries outside the US where Hip-Hop is most popular is the United Kingdom. In the 2000s a derivative genre from Hip-Hop (as well as UK Garage and Drum and Bass) known as Grime became popular with artists such as Dizzee Rascal becoming successful. Although it is immensely popular, many British politicians criticize the music for what they see as promoting theft and murder, similar to gangsta rap in America. These criticisms have been deemed racist by the mostly Black British grime industry. Despite its controversial nature, grime has had a major affect on British fashion and pop music, with many young working class youth emulating the clothing worn by grime stars like Dizzee Rascal and Wiley. There are many subgenres of grime, including Rhythm and Grime, a mix of R&B and grime, and grindie, a mix of indie rock and grime popularized by indie rock band Hadouken.

Rap has globalized into many cultures worldwide, as evident through the emergence of numerous regional scenes. It has emerged globally as a movement based upon the main tennets of hip hop culture. The music and the art continue to embrace, even celebrate, its transnational dimensions while staying true to the local cultures to which it is rooted. Hip-hop's inspiration differs depending on each culture. Still, the one thing virtually all Hip Hop artists worldwide have in common is that they acknowledge their debt to African Americans in the state of New York who launched the global movement. While hip-hop is sometimes taken for granted by Americans, it is not so elsewhere, especially in the developing world, where it has come to represent the empowerment of the disenfranchised and a slice of the American dream. American Hip-Hop music has reached the cultural corridors of the globe and has been absorbed and reinvented around the world.

GLITCH HOP AND WONKY MUSIC

Glitch Hop and Wonky music evolved following the rise of Trip Hop, dubstep and IDM. Both styles of music frequently reflect the experimental nature of IDM and the heavy bass featured in dubstep songs. While trip hop was described as being a distinct British upper-middle class take on Hip-Hop, glitch-hop and wonky music have featured much more stylistic diversity. Both genres are melting pots of influence, echoes of 80s pop music, Indian ragas, eclectic jazz, and West Coast rap can be heard in Glitch Hop productions. Los Angeles, London, Glasgow and a number of other cities have become hot spots for these scenes, and underground scenes have developed across the world in smaller communities. Both genres often pay homage to more well older and more well established electronic music artists such as Radiohead, Aphex Twin and Boards of Canada as well as independent hip hop producers like J Dilla and Madlib.

Glitch Hop is a fusion genre of hip hop and glitch music that originated in the early to mid 2000s in the United States and Europe. Musically, it is based on irregular, chaotic breakbeats, glitchy basslines and other typical sound effects used in glitch music, like skips. Glitch Hop artists include Prefuse Dabrye and Flying Lotus.

CRUNK AND SNAP MUSIC

Crunk originated from southern hip hop in the late 1990s. The style was pioneered and commercialized by artists from Memphis, Tennessee, and Atlanta, Georgia. Looped, stripped-down drum machine rhythms are usually used. The Roland TR-808 and 909 are among the most popular. The drum machines are usually accompanied by simple, repeated synthesizer melodies and heavy bass stabs. The tempo of the music is somewhat slower than hip-hop, around the speed of reggaeton.

The focal point of crunk is more often the beats and music than the lyrics therein. Crunk rappers, however, often shout and scream their lyrics, creating an aggressive, almost heavy, style of hip-hop. While other subgenres of hip-hop address sociopolitical or personal concerns, crunk is almost exclusively party music, favoring call and response hip-hop slogans in lieu of more substantive approaches.

WHAT TO READ NEXT...

Trap didn't end because you finished this book.
Go back and read how it all came about...

Volume One

Volume Two

Volume Three

Volume Four

Volume Five

For media inquiries, foreign rights, inquiries, promotions, or just need want to drop me a shoutout!

email: feekness@gmail.com

www.ingramcontent.com/pod-product-compliance
Lightning Source LLC
Chambersburg PA
CBHW071754080526
44588CB00013B/2230